white cloud

blue balloon

yellow chick

red boots

pink dessert

Numbers

can you count from 1 to 5?

1 **one**

How many flowers can you see?

two

2

How many fish are swimming?

3 ●●●

three

How many balls
is the clown
juggling?

four

4 ●●●●

How many candles
are on the cake?

five

5 ●●●●●

How many shells are there?

Shapes

Everything is made of shapes. Can you see any of these shapes in your home?

What shape is the book?

 a rectangle

a circle ○ What shape is the dog's ball?

a star

What shape is the top
of the fairy's wand?

a square

What shape is the window?

What shape is
the sail?

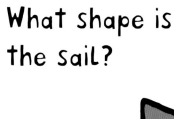

a triangle

Opposites

The opposite of **happy** is **Sad**.
Here are some more opposites:

The bowl is **hard**.

The kitten's fur is **soft**.

up

The see-saw
moves **up**
and **down**.

down

This horse is **big**.

This horse is **small**.

The rabbit is **in** the hat.

The rabbit is **out** of the hat.

This teddy bear's tie is **short**.

This teddy bear's tie is **long**.

First Words

Look around your home and try
to find some of these things.

brush

comb

mirror

bed

doll